THE LITTLE BOOK OF
BOOKS

Published in 2022 by OH!
An Imprint of Welbeck Non-Fiction Limited,
part of Welbeck Publishing Group.
Based in London and Sydney.
www.welbeckpublishing.com

Compilation text © Welbeck Non-Fiction Limited 2022
Design © Welbeck Non-Fiction Limited 2022

ISBN 978-1-80069-174-2

Compiled and written by: Marcus Leaver
Editorial: Stella Caldwell
Project manager: Russell Porter
Design: Tony Seddon
Production: Jess Brisley

A CIP catalogue record for this book is available from the British Library

Printed in China

10 9 8 7 6 5 4 3 2 1

Illustrations: Freepik.com

THE LITTLE BOOK OF
BOOKS

QUOTES FOR THE BIBLIOPHILE
IN YOUR LIFE

CONTENTS

This book is dedicated to Henry,
a dear friend, who was
amused by the choice of author
and this publication.

Dear Book Lover

It was a joy to collate more than 200 one-liners, quotes about books, and great lines from great works to put into this small but perfectly formed little book about books and reading. I have enjoyed every minute of choosing what to include and what to discard.

Of course, this book is just my take on the subject and the pleasure it gives me. As with any curation, you will be pleased to revisit some much-loved lines, and disappointed that others you closely identify with have been left out. But hopefully, the bibliophile will find something contained within these pages to delight them, inspire them or have them buy another book, for themselves or as a gift for someone dear to them.

HAPPY READING.

Marcus E. Leaver
London
July 2021

CHAPTER

1

One-liners

*Do you live for books?
Do you believe that a room
without books is like a body
without a soul? Do you think
books should be tasted….?*

*What follows are some of my
favourite quotes by some of the
most famous people who have
ever lived and written.*

66

We live for books.

99

Umberto Eco

> **"**
>
> # Books are a uniquely portable magic.
>
> **"**
>
> *Stephen King*

66

A room without books is like a body without a soul.

99

Cicero

Good friends,
good books,
and a sleepy
conscience: this
is the ideal life.

Mark Twain

Books serve to show a man that those original thoughts of his aren't very new after all.

Abraham Lincoln

Some books should
be tasted, some
devoured, but only
a few should be
chewed and digested
thoroughly.

Sir Francis Bacon

Let us read and let us dance; these two amusements will never do any harm to the world.

Voltaire

You cannot open a book without learning something.

Confucius

> Read the best books first, or you may not have a chance to read them at all.

Henry David Thoreau

Classic – a book
which people
praise and
don't read.

Mark Twain

Books are the training weights of the mind.

Epictetus

I have never
known any
distress that an
hour's reading
did not relieve.

Montesquieu

To read without reflecting is like eating without digesting.

Edmund Burke

The most technologically efficient machine that man has ever invented is the book.

Northrop Frye

A book is a gift you can open again and again.

Garrison Keillor

To learn to read
is to light a fire;
every syllable
that is spelled out
is a spark.

Victor Hugo

A house without
books is like a
room without
windows.

Heinrich Mann

Show me a family of readers, and I will show you the people who move the world.

Napoleon Bonaparte

No entertainment
is so cheap
as reading, nor
any pleasure so
lasting.

Mary Wortley Montagu

The reading of all good books is like a conversation with the finest minds of past centuries.

René Descartes

That's the thing about books. They let you travel without moving your feet.

Jhumpa Lahiri

A reader lives a thousand lives before he dies.

George R.R. Martin

I do believe
something very
magical can
happen when you
read a good book.

J.K. Rowling

The only thing you absolutely have to know is the location of the library.

Albert Einstein

An hour spent reading is one stolen from paradise.

Thomas Wharton

Reading is an active, imaginative act; it takes work.

Khaled Hosseini

> People don't realize how a man's whole life can be changed by one book.

Malcolm X

> ## Of all things, I liked books best.

Nikola Tesla

I kept always
two books in my
pocket, one
to read, one to
write in.

Robert Louis Stevenson

> Think before you speak, read before you think.

Fran Lebowitz

Only a
generation
of readers
will spawn a
generation of
writers.

Steven Spielberg

Once you have
read a book you
care about, some
part of it is always
with you.

Louis L'Amour

Not all readers are leaders, but all leaders are readers.

Harry S. Truman

The world is a hellish place, and bad writing is destroying the quality of our suffering.

Tom Waits

66
Beware the person of a single book.

99

Thomas Aquinas

Reading is to the mind what exercise is to the body.

Joseph Addison

The person who deserves most pity is a lonesome one on a rainy day who doesn't know how to read.

Benjamin Franklin

A book is a device to ignite the imagination.

Alan Bennett

A good book is an
event in my life.

Stendhal

I think books are like
people, in the sense
that they'll turn up
in your life when you
most need them.

Emma Thompson

CHAPTER

2

The Magic of Books

*Books are truly magical.
They can entertain you, inspire
you, educate you – and,
always, they can enrich your
life in some way.*

*Some wise words follow about
that very magic.*

Books may
well be the only
true magic.

Alice Hoffman

66

A great book should
leave you with many
experiences, and
slightly exhausted
at the end. You live
several lives while
reading.

99

William Styron

In the case of good books, the point is not to see how many of them you can get through, but rather how many can get through to you.

Mortimer J. Adler

I can never read all the books
I want; I can never be all
the people I want and live all the
lives I want. I can never train
myself in all the skills I want.
And why do I want?
I want to live and feel all the
shades, tones and variations of
mental and physical experience
possible in my life. And I am
horribly limited.

Sylvia Plath

Whenever you
read a good book,
somewhere in the
world a door opens to
allow in more light.

Vera Nazarian

66

Second-hand books
are wild books, homeless
books; they have come
together in vast flocks of
variegated feather and
have a charm which the
domesticated volumes
of the library lack.

99

Virginia Woolf

It is not true that we have only one life to live; if we can read, we can live as many more lives and as many kinds of lives as we wish.

S.I. Hayakawa

> We don't need a list of rights and wrongs, tables of dos and don'ts: we need books, time, and silence. Thou shalt not is soon forgotten, but Once upon a time lasts forever.

Philip Pullman

Books and doors
are the same thing.
You open them, and
you go through into
another world.

Jeanette Winterson

"

Of course, anyone who
truly loves books buys more
of them than he or she can
hope to read in one fleeting
lifetime. A good book,
resting unopened in its slot
on a shelf, full of majestic
potentiality, is the most
comforting sort of intellectual
wallpaper.

"

David Quammen

I'm old-fashioned
and think that
reading books is the
most glorious pastime
that humankind has
yet devised.

Wisława Szymborska

Read a lot. Expect something big, something exalting or deepening from a book. No book is worth reading that isn't worth re-reading.

Susan Sontag

There is nothing more luxurious than eating while you read – unless it be reading while you eat.

E. Nesbit

Man reading should
be man intensely
alive. The book
should be a ball of
light in one's hand.

Ezra Pound

Books are not made
for furniture, but
there is nothing else
that so beautifully
furnishes a house.

Henry Ward Beecher

Books are the quietest
and most constant of
friends; they are the most
accessible and wisest of
counsellors, and the most
patient of teachers.

Charles William Eliot

Just the knowledge
that a good book
is awaiting one
at the end of a long
day makes that
day happier.

Kathleen Norris

If you would tell
me the heart of a
man, tell me not
what he reads, but
what he re-reads.

François Mauriac

Many people,
myself among them,
feel better at the
mere sight of a book.

Jane Smiley

When we are
collecting books,
we are collecting
happiness.

Vincent Starrett

66

Everything in the world exists in order to end up as a book.

99

Stéphane Mallarmé

> ## It does not do to dwell on dreams and forget to live.

J.K. Rowling,
Harry Potter and The Sorcerer's Stone

CHAPTER

3

The Power
of Words
and Writing

*Writing is never as easy
as it seems. But books are
knowledge, books are reflection
and books change your mind.*

*Some celebrated authors
explain why.*

Books are a form of
political action.
Books are knowledge.
Books are reflection.
Books change your
mind.

Toni Morrison

A word after a word after a word is power.

Margaret Atwood

Despite the enormous quantity of books, how few people read! And if one reads profitably, one would realize how much stupid stuff the vulgar herd is content to swallow every day.

Voltaire

Writing books is the closest men ever come to childbearing.

Norman Mailer

To produce a mighty book, you must choose a mighty theme.

Herman Melville

66

A blank piece
of paper is God's
way of telling us
how hard it is
to be God.

99

Sidney Sheldon

"

I love
deadlines. I like
the whooshing
sound they make
as they fly by.

"

Douglas Adams

There is no greater agony than bearing an untold story inside you.

Maya Angelou

The English language is
an arsenal of weapons. If
you are going to brandish
them without checking
to see whether or not
they are loaded, you must
expect to have them
explode in your face
from time to time.

Stephen Fry

If my doctor told me I had only six minutes to live, I wouldn't brood. I'd type a little faster.

Isaac Asimov

66

Reading is my
inhale, and
writing is my
exhale.

99

Glennon Doyle

There are three rules
for writing the
novel. Unfortunately,
no one knows what
they are.

W. Somerset Maugham

No tears in the writer, no tears in the reader. No surprise in the writer, no surprise in the reader.

Robert Frost

A writer only begins a book. A reader finishes it.

Samuel Johnson

66

Reading is the finest teacher of how to write.

99

Annie Proulx

Libraries will get
you through times
of no money better
than money will get
you through times
of no libraries.

Anne Herbert

> I couldn't live a week
> without a private library –
> indeed, I'd part with
> all my furniture and
> squat and sleep on the
> floor before I'd let go
> of the 1,500 or so books,
> I possess.

H. P. Lovecraft

When I am attacked by gloomy thoughts, nothing helps me so much as running to my books. They quickly absorb me and banish the clouds from my mind.

Michel de Montaigne

Words dazzle and deceive because they are mimed by the face. But black words on a white page are the soul laid bare.

Guy de Maupassant

> **Even today, when I read, I notice with pleasure when an author has chosen a particular word, a particular place, for the picture it will convey to the reader.**

Ruth Bader Ginsburg

I don't believe one reads to escape reality. A person reads to confirm a reality he knows is there, but which he has not experienced.

Lawrence Durrell

66

Do not read, as children do, to amuse yourself, or like the ambitious, for the purpose of instruction. No, read in order to live.

99

Gustave Flaubert

Employ your
time in improving
yourself by other
men's writings so that
you shall come easily
by what others have
laboured hard for.

Socrates

> I know nothing in the world that has as much power as a word. Sometimes I write one, and I look at it, until it begins to shine.

Emily Dickinson

The best advice
I ever got was that
knowledge is power
and to keep reading.

David Bailey

Beware; for I am fearless, and therefore powerful.

Mary Shelley, Frankenstein

CHAPTER

4

A Precious Gift

*A child who is read to
or receives a book will never
see reading as a chore but as
a precious gift.*

*And when that child grows
into an adult, they can keep
that precious gift for life.*

Reading should not be presented to children as a chore or duty. It should be offered to them as a precious gift.

Kate DiCamillo

A children's story that
can only be enjoyed
by children is not a
good children's story
in the slightest.

C.S. Lewis

I wouldn't be a songwriter if it wasn't for books that I loved as a kid. I think that when you can escape into a book it trains your imagination to think big and to think that more can exist than what you see.

Taylor Swift

Reading is the gateway skill that makes all other learning possible.

Barack Obama

There are many
little ways to enlarge
your child's world.
Love of books is
the best of all.

Jacqueline Kennedy

Once you learn to read, you will be forever free.

Frederick Douglass

66

There are perhaps no days of our childhood we lived so fully as those we spent with a favourite book.

99

Marcel Proust

One child, one teacher, one book and one pen can change the world.

Malala Yousafzai

Reading is important, because if you can read, you can learn anything about everything and everything about anything.

Tomie dePaola

66

I have a passion for teaching
kids to become readers,
to become comfortable with
a book, not daunted.
Books shouldn't be daunting,
they should be funny, exciting
and wonderful; and
learning to be a reader gives
a terrific advantage.

99

Roald Dahl

Books to the ceiling,
Books to the sky,
My pile of books is a
mile high.
How I love them!
How I need them!
I'll have a long beard by
the time I read them.

Arnold Lobel

Fairy tales don't tell children that dragons exist… Fairy tales tell children that dragons can be killed.

G.K. Chesterton

There is no substitute for books in the life of a child.

Mary Ellen Chase

There's no such thing as a kid who hates reading. There are kids who love reading, and kids who are reading the wrong books.

James Patterson

"If you want your children to be intelligent, read them fairy tales. If you want them to be more intelligent, read them more fairy tales."

Albert Einstein

Always read something that will make you look good if you die in the middle of it.

P.J. O'Rourke

Outside of a dog, a book is man's best friend. Inside of a dog it's too dark to read.

Groucho Marx, The Essential Groucho

Fill your house
with stacks of
books, in all the
crannies and all
the nooks.

Dr. Seuss

There are two motives for reading a book: one, that you enjoy it; the other, that you can boast about it.

Bertrand Russell, The Conquest of Happiness

66

A bookstore is
one of the many
pieces of evidence
we have that
people are still
thinking.

99

Jerry Seinfeld

Let's be reasonable
and add an eighth day
to the week that is
devoted exclusively
to reading.

Lena Dunham

To a soul attuned to the subtle rhythms of a library, there are few worse sights than a hole where a book ought to be.

Terry Pratchett

> Never lend books, for no one ever returns them; the only books I have in my library are books that other folks have lent me.

Anatole France

> **"**
>
> I love walking into
> a bookstore.
> It's like all my friends
> are sitting on
> shelves, waving their
> pages at me.
>
> **"**

Tahereh Mafi

"

Take a good
book to bed with
you – books do
not snore.

Thea Dorn

What I say is, a town
isn't a town without
a bookstore.
It may call itself a town,
but unless it's got
a bookstore, it knows
it's not foolin' a soul.

Neil Gaiman, American Gods

There are books of which the backs and covers are by far the best parts.

Charles Dickens, Oliver Twist

The reason that fiction is
more interesting than any
other form of literature,
to those who really like to
study people, is that in fiction
the author can really tell
the truth without humiliating
himself.

Eleanor Roosevelt

Where is human nature so weak as in the bookstore?

Henry Ward Beecher

I read my eyes
out and can't read
half enough…
The more one reads
the more one sees we
have to read.

John Adams

People can
lose their lives
in libraries.
They ought to
be warned.

Saul Bellow

Oh, the places you'll go! You'll be on your way up! You'll be seeing great sights! You'll join the high-fliers who soar to high heights.

Dr. Seuss, Oh, the Places You'll Go

CHAPTER

5

Mirrors of
the Soul

In the same way every book is
different, what a book means to each
and every person can be different.

Where were you when you
read the book? Who were you with?
Were you happy or sad?
Energetic or tired? Are there any
evocative smells or sounds
that rush back when you think
of that book?

66

Books are the mirrors of the soul.

99

Virginia Woolf

66

One glance at a
book and you hear the
voice of another person,
perhaps someone
dead for 1,000 years.
To read is to voyage
through time.

99

Carl Sagan

You can never
get a cup of tea
large enough or a
book long enough
to suit me.

C.S. Lewis

> If one cannot
> enjoy reading a
> book over and
> over again, there
> is no use in
> reading it at all.

Oscar Wilde

There is more treasure in books than in all the pirate's loot on Treasure Island.

Walt Disney

66

And read…
read all the time…
read as a matter of
principle, as a matter
of self-respect.
Read as a nourishing
staple of life.

99

David McCullough Jr.

Books were my pass to personal freedom.

Oprah Winfrey

More than at any
other time, when
I hold a beloved
book in my hand my
limitations fall from
me, my spirit is free.

Helen Keller

Reading is escape, and the opposite of escape; it's a way to make contact with reality after a day of making things up, and it's a way of making contact with someone else's imagination after a day that's all too real.

Nora Ephron

For some of us, books are as important as almost anything else on earth. What a miracle it is that out of these small, flat, rigid squares of paper unfolds world after world after world, worlds that sing to you, comfort and quiet or excite you. Books help us understand who we are and how we are to behave. They show us what community and friendship mean; they show us how to live and die.

Anne Lamott

What a blessing it
is to love books as
I love them; to be
able to converse with
the dead, and to live
amidst the unreal!

Thomas Babington Macaulay

66

Reading is an
exercise in empathy;
an exercise in
walking in someone
else's shoes for
a while.

99

Malorie Blackman

Maybe this is why
we read, and why in
moments of darkness
we return to books:
to find words for what
we already know.

Alberto Manguel

The unread story
is not a story; it is
little black marks on
wood pulp.
The reader, reading
it, makes it live: a live
thing, a story.

Ursula K. LeGuin

Reading is an act of
civilization; it's one of the
greatest acts of civilization
because it takes the free
raw material of the mind
and builds castles of
possibilities.

Ben Okri

Books are mirrors:
you only see in them
what you already
have inside you.

Carlos Ruiz Zafón,
The Shadow of the Wind

Reading makes immigrants of us all. It takes us away from home, but more important, it finds homes for us everywhere.

Jean Rhys

The best moments in reading are
when you come across something –
a thought, a feeling, a way of looking
at things – which you had thought
special and particular to you.
Now here it is, set down by someone
else, a person you have never met,
someone even who is long dead.
And it is as if a hand has come out
and taken yours.

Alan Bennett, The History Boys

If you cannot read all your books... fondle them, peer into them, let them fall open where they will, read from the first sentence that arrests the eye, set them back on the shelves with your own hands, arrange them on your own plan so that you at least know where they are. Let them be your friends; let them, at any rate, be your acquaintances.

Winston Churchill

66

To acquire the habit
of reading is to
construct for yourself
a refuge from almost
all the miseries
of life.

99

W. Somerset Maugham

Read, read, read.
Read everything — trash,
classics, good and bad, and
see how they do it. Just like
a carpenter who works as an
apprentice and studies the
master. Read! You'll absorb it.
Then write. If it's good, you'll
find out. If it's not, throw it
out of the window.

William Faulkner

Books give a soul to
the universe, wings to
the mind, flight to the
imagination, and life
to everything.

Plato

When I think about
how I understand my
role as citizen, setting
aside being president...
the most important stuff
I've learned I think I've
learned from novels.

Barack Obama

"
We are such stuff as
dreams are made on,
and our little life is
rounded with a sleep.
"

William Shakespeare, The Tempest

CHAPTER

6

Famous Lines from Famous Books

What follows are some of my favourite lines from well-known books I have read.

Hopefully you'll find some pixie dust, and, if you do, don't procrastinate – make a list of your own from the books you love.

I declare after all there is no enjoyment like reading! How much sooner one tires of anything than of a book! When I have a house of my own, I shall be miserable if I have not an excellent library.

Jane Austen, Pride and Prejudice

> 66
>
> If you only read the books that everyone else is reading, you can only think what everyone else is thinking.
>
> 99
>
> *Haruki Murakami*, Norwegian Wood

Who controls the past controls the future. Who controls the present controls the past.

George Orwell, Nineteen Eighty-Four

It is better to know one book intimately than a hundred superficially.

Donna Tartt, The Secret History

What really knocks me out
is a book that, when you're all
done reading it, you wish the
author that wrote it was a
terrific friend of yours
and you could call him up
on the phone whenever
you felt like it. That doesn't
happen much, though.

J.D. Salinger, The Catcher In The Rye

66

Some of these
things are true
and some of them
lies. But they are
all good stories.

99

Hilary Mantel, Wolf Hall

Until I feared
I would lose it,
I never loved
to read.
One does not
love breathing.

Harper Lee, To Kill A Mockingbird

The magic is only in what books say, how they stitched the patches of the universe together into one garment for us.

Ray Bradbury, Fahrenheit 451

A classic is a successful
book that has survived the
reaction of the next period
or generation. Then it's safe,
like a style in architecture
or furniture. It's acquired a
picturesque dignity to take
the place of its fashion.

F. Scott Fitzgerald, The Beautiful and Damned

All the world
is made of faith,
and trust, and
pixie dust.

J.M Barrie, Peter Pan

A man, after he has brushed off the dust and chips of his life, will have left only the hard, clean questions: Was it good or was it evil? Have I done well – or ill?

John Steinbeck, East of Eden

66

I am no bird; and no
net ensnares me:
I am a free human
being with an
independent will,
which I now exert to
leave you.

99

Charlotte Brontë, Jane Eyre

Some books
are so familiar
that reading them
is like being
home again.

Louisa May Alcott, Little Women

As I left China farther and farther behind, I looked out of the window and saw a great universe beyond the plane's silver wing. I took one more glance over my past life, then turned to the future. I was eager to embrace the world.

Jung Chang, Wild Swans

'Why did you do all this for me?' he asked. 'I don't deserve it. I've never done anything for you.' 'You have been my friend,' replied Charlotte. 'That in itself is a tremendous thing.'

E.B. White, Charlotte's Web

It is nothing to die; it is dreadful not to live.

Victor Hugo, Les Miserables

All happy families
are alike; each
unhappy family
is unhappy in its
own way.

Leo Tolstoy, Anna Karenina

Memories warm you up from the inside. But they also tear you apart.

Haruki Murakami, Kafka on the Shore

It was the best of times, it was the worst of times, it was the age of wisdom, it was the age of foolishness, it was the epoch of belief, it was the epoch of incredulity, it was the season of Light, it was the season of Darkness, it was the spring of hope, it was the winter of despair...

Charles Dickens, A Tale of Two Cities

Why, sometimes, I've believed as many as six impossible things before breakfast.

Lewis Carroll, Through the Looking Glass

66

If you have the guts to be yourself, other people'll pay your price.

99

John Updike, Rabbit, Run

Generally, by the time you are Real, most of your hair has been loved off, and your eyes drop out and you get loose in the joints and very shabby. But these things don't matter at all, because once you are Real you can't be ugly, except to people who don't understand.

Margery Williams, The Velveteen Rabbit

Love is the longing for the half of ourselves we have lost.

Milan Kundera,
The Unbearable Lightness of Being

> ## My advice is, never do tomorrow what you can do today. Procrastination is the thief of time.

Charles Dickens, David Copperfield

66

It is only with the
heart that one can
see rightly; what is
essential is invisible
to the eye.

99

Antoine de Saint-Exupéry,
The Little Prince

'And now,' cried
Max, 'let the wild
rumpus start!'

Maurice Sendak,
Where the Wild Things Are

Memories, even your
most precious ones, fade
surprisingly quickly.
But I don't go along with
that. The memories
I value most, I don't ever
see them fading.

Kazuo Ishiguro, Never Let Me Go

But wherever they go,
and whatever happens to
them on the way, in that
enchanted place on the
top of the Forest a
little boy and his Bear will
always be playing.

A.A. Milne,
The House At Pooh Corner

The old man
was dreaming
about the lions.

Ernest Hemingway,
The Old Man and the Sea